Collins

GCSE Home Economics
Child
Development
for AQA

Student Workbook

Janet Stearns and Mark Walsh

Published by Collins Learning
An imprint of HarperCollins*Publishers*
77–85 Fulham Palace Road
Hammersmith
London
W6 8JB

Browse the complete Collins Education catalogue at
www.collinseducation.com

ISBN-13 978-0-00-735057-5
Janet Stearns and Mark Walsh assert the moral right to be identified as the
authors of this work.

British Library Cataloguing in Publication Data
A Catalogue record for this publication is available from the British Library.

Commissioned by Emma Woolf
Project managed by Jo Kemp
Edited by Gudrun Kaiser
Picture research by Geoff Holdsworth/Picturesearch.co.uk
Text design by Thomson Digital/G. Brasnett
Layout by G. Brasnett, Cambridge
Cover design by Angela English
Artwork by Jerry Fowler

Acknowledgements
iStockphoto (5/H-Gall); iStockphoto (19/Max Delson Martins Santos);
iStockphoto (38/Nagy-Bagoly Ilona); iStockphoto (52/Yvonne Chamberlain);
iStockphoto (59/Christopher Futcher).
Every effort has been made to contact copyright holders, but if any have been
inadvertently overlooked, the publishers will be pleased to make the necessary
arrangements at the first opportunity.

Contents

Introduction

This workbook is made up of questions and activities that cover each section of the AQA GCSE Home Economics (Child Development) specification. The questions and activities are designed to develop and assess your knowledge and understanding of a range of topics that are part of the GCSE award. To get the most out of using this workbook as part of your GCSE course, you need to understand the following points.

▶ What you learn from studying the course with your class tutor and from using a textbook written for the AQA GCSE Home Economics (Child Development) qualification will provide you with the background knowledge needed to complete the questions and activities in this workbook.

▶ You should complete the questions and activities after you have studied the corresponding part of the course using textbooks and other resources with your tutor or as your tutor directs.

▶ It is best to complete the questions and activities for each section before you begin any of the controlled assessment tasks for the course. Completing the questions and activities to the best of your ability will help to prepare you for these important assessments.

▶ The mark allocations and the number of answer lines provided for each question or activity are a guide as to how much to write in your answer.

▶ Questions that require you to provide a specific number of examples ('Give three examples of...') or to identify a specific number of reasons ('Describe two reasons why...'), your answer must provide the specified number of items to achieve full marks. Providing more examples or more reasons than required will not gain you any more marks, so it is best not to do this.

When AQA sets controlled assessment tasks and assignment questions they choose the words very carefully. You need to remember that the way a question is asked, or a task is worded, is very important. Always make sure that you read, understand and respond to the command verb – for example, 'describe', 'explain' – in order to get the right level of detail in your answer. 'Name' and 'give' are low level question verbs for 1 or 2 marks; 'describe' usually requires more detail for 2 or more marks; 'explain' typically requires even more detail, and 'evaluate' requires the most detail.

Finally, when answering questions, make sure that you write clearly and spell correctly. This is vital when using the specialist words and phrases of the child development field.

1 Parenthood

This chapter covers the following topics:

1.1   The family

1.2   Planning for a family

1.3   Preparing for the baby

1.4   Provision of a safe environment

Before you complete the questions in this chapter, begin any controlled assessment tasks, or sit any exam questions related to *Parenthood*, you will need to have learned about:

▶   the importance of the family unit

▶   the variation in family types, structures and lifestyles in a multicultural society

▶   the factors to consider when planning a family

▶   the factors to consider when choosing clothing and equipment for a new baby

▶   the importance of safety with babies and young children

▶   some of the common causes of accidents, both indoors and outdoors, and ways to prevent them happening

▶   some simple first aid treatments for children.

The questions and activities that follow provide you with an opportunity to develop your knowledge and assess your understanding of the range of topics that are part of this chapter.

Topic 1.1 The family

The main issues covered in this topic are:

▶ the importance of the family in providing for the child's basic needs

▶ the variation in family types and structures in a multicultural society

▶ the nature of changing roles and responsibilities within families

▶ the advantages and disadvantages of different family types.

Refer to the work you have completed in class or to your course textbook if you are unsure about any of the topics covered by these questions, or if you need to remind yourself of the main points.

Questions and activities

A family is a group of people who live together or who are related by blood ties, marriage or adoption. There is a diverse range of family structures in the UK today.

1. Name *four* types of family structures present in the UK today. **(4 marks)**

   i) _____

   ii) _____

   iii) _____

   iv) _____

2. Explain the term 'adoptive family' and identify how this differs from a 'foster family'. **(3 marks)**

_____

_____

_____

_____

_____

_____

The modern family performs a number of important functions for its members.

3. Describe *three* ways that the modern family promotes child development. **(3 marks)**

_____

_____

_____

_____

_____

_____

4. What does the term 'socialisation' mean? **(2 marks)**

_____

_____

_____

_____

5. Describe _two_ things that families do to socialise young children. **(2 marks)**

i) _____

_____

ii) _____

_____

Family structures have changed significantly over the last 50 years. The UK now has a diverse range of family types. One major change has been the decline in the number of extended family households in the UK.

6. What are the main characteristics of the 'extended family'? **(3 marks)**

_____

_____

_____

7. Describe _four_ reasons for the decline in the number of extended families in the UK over the last 50 years.
   (4 marks)

i) _____

_____

_____

ii) _____

_____

_____

iii) _____

_____

_____

iv) _____

_____

_____

Debbie has been married twice. She had one child with each ex-husband. Debbie is now divorced and cohabiting with Simon. Debbie and Simon have a child of their own. Debbie, Simon and the three children live together in the same household and consider themselves to be a 'blended' or 'reconstituted' family.

8. Describe the main characteristics of a blended or reconstituted family. **(4 marks)**

_____

_____

_____

_____

_____

_____

9. Give _three_ reasons for the growth in the number of blended families in the UK over the last 30 years. **(3 marks)**

i) _____

_____

ii) _____

_____

iii) _____

_____

10. Explain how roles and responsibilities have changed within the family over the last 20 years and identify the possible benefits of two of these changes for children's development. **(6 marks)**

_____

_____

_____

_____

_____

_____

_____

_____

_____

_____

_____

_____

_____

When children are unable to live with their birth or adoptive families, they are usually looked after by local authorities who provide residential care homes for children.

11. What is a 'local authority'? **(1 mark)**

_____

_____

12. Give *four* reasons why a child may be unable to live with his or her family. **(4 marks)**

i) _____

ii) _____

iii) _____

iv) _____

The number of children looked after by local authorities in residential children's homes has declined significantly since the 1970s.

13. Explain why there are now far fewer children living in residential children's homes in the UK than there were in the 1970s. **(4 marks)**

_____

_____

_____

_____

_____

_____

14. Complete the table below by giving *four* arguments in favour of and *four* criticisms of residential childcare for vulnerable children. **(8 marks)**

Arguments in favour	Criticisms
i)	i)
ii)	ii)
iii)	iii)
iv)	iv)

Eva is 3 years of age. Her mum, a lone parent, has been admitted to hospital with a serious infection. As a result, Eva has been taken into care by her local authority. They have identified a foster family who will look after Eva until her mum is well.

15. Describe the role and responsibilities of Eva's foster parents. **(4 marks)**

_____

_____

_____

_____

_____

_____

_____

_____

16. Give *three* reasons why fostering may be the best way of providing care for Eva in the circumstances described. **(3 marks)**

i) _____

_____

ii) _____

_____

iii) _____

_____

17. Explain the differences between adoption and fostering. **(6 marks)**

_____

_____

_____

_____

_____

_____

_____

_____

_____

_____

_____

_____

Charlie and Hattie cannot have children of their own due to fertility problems. They have approached their local authority about adopting a baby or child under the age of 3 years.

18. Describe the emotional benefits for a child, of being adopted by a couple like Charlie and Hattie, rather than being fostered or looked after in long-term residential care by a local authority. **(3 marks)**

_____

_____

_____

_____

_____

_____

_____

_____

_____

_____

19. Explain why couples may wish to adopt a child, and what rights and responsibilities they will have for the child if they are successful. **(6 marks)**

_____

_____

_____

_____

_____

_____

_____

_____

_____

_____

_____

_____

_____

_____

_____

_____

_____

Topic 1.2 Planning for a family

The main issues covered in this topic are:

▶ the factors a couple need to think about in preparation for becoming parents

▶ the impact a child can have on a couple's relationship and lifestyle

▶ the lifestyle choices and health issues that a couple should consider when deciding to become parents.

Refer to the work you have completed in class or to your course textbook if you are unsure about any of the topics covered by these questions, or if you need to remind yourself of the main points.

Questions and activities

1. Explain why the following factors are important when a couple are deciding to have a baby. **(4 marks)**

   a) A secure, stable relationship

   _____

   _____

   _____

   b) Realistic expectations about the changes a baby makes to one's lifestyle

   _____

   _____

   _____

2. Identify two other lifestyle factors that a couple should consider before deciding to have a baby. **(2 marks)**

   i) _____

   ii) _____

> Some couples may decide to start a family when they are young; others may wait until they are older.

3. Complete the table below, listing two advantages and two disadvantages of being young parents and of being older parents. **(8 marks)**

Age of parents	Advantages	Disadvantages
Young	i) ii)	i) ii)
Older	i) ii)	i) ii)

Karl is 27 years old and Joanna is 25. They have been married for two years and are planning to start a family. Joanna works part time as a receptionist and Karl is in full-time employment. Karl smokes about 20 cigarettes a day and Joanna is vegetarian. They live in a small, one-bedroom flat, which is near a busy road and has no garden.

4. Explain why it is important for Karl and Joanna to plan their family. **(3 marks)**

_____

_____

_____

_____

_____

_____

5. Describe two important decisions that Karl and Joanna might have to make before deciding to have a baby. **(4 marks)**

i) _____

_____

ii) _____

_____

Topic 1.3 Preparing for the baby

The main issues covered in this topic include:

▶ the essential clothing and equipment needed for a new baby

▶ the factors to consider when choosing clothing and equipment for a new baby.

Refer to the work you have completed in class or to your course textbook if you are unsure about any of the topics covered by these questions, or if you need to remind yourself of the main points.

Questions and activities

1. Explain what you understand by the term 'layette'. **(1 mark)**

_____

_____

2. Identify _five_ essential items that you think might be included in a new baby's layette. **(5 marks)**

i) _____

ii) _____

iii) _____

iv) _____

v) _____

It is important to prepare clothing and equipment for a new baby. Nappies are essential for new babies and can be disposable or reusable. There are advantages and disadvantages to both types.

3. Complete the following table. **(12 marks)**

Type of nappy	Advantages	Disadvantages
Disposable	i) _____ ii) _____ iii) _____	i) _____ ii) _____ iii) _____
Reusable	i) _____ ii) _____ iii) _____	i) _____ ii) _____ iii) _____

Imagine that you are a sales assistant in a store that sells baby clothes and equipment. Your job is to advise parents-to-be when they visit the store to buy clothing and equipment for their new baby.

4. What advice would you give to expectant parents who want to buy the following items? **(8 marks)**

a) A pram for their new baby.

_____
_____
_____
_____
_____
_____
_____

b) Clothing for their new baby.

_____
_____
_____
_____
_____
_____
_____

Topic 1.4 Provision of a safe environment

The main issues covered in this topic are:

▶ how to identify a range of hazards and risks to young children

▶ reasons why babies and young children sometimes experience accidents

▶ how to reduce the risks of accidents occurring

▶ simple first aid treatments for minor accidents and injuries.

Refer to the work you have completed in class or to your course textbook if you are unsure about any of the topics covered by these questions, or if you need to remind yourself of the main points.

Questions and activities

1. Use an example related to playing in the garden to explain the following terms. **(4 marks)**

    a) Hazard: _____

    _____

    _____

    _____

    b) Risk: _____

    _____

    _____

    _____

A kitchen can be a dangerous place for a young child.

2. Identify *four* hazards to a young child's safety that can be found in domestic kitchens. **(4 marks)**

    i) _____

    ii) _____

    iii) _____

    iv) _____

3. Identify *four* items of safety equipment that can be used to reduce the risk of kitchen hazards to children. **(4 marks)**

    i) _____

    ii) _____

    iii) _____

    iv) _____

4. Explain why babies, toddlers and young children are at risk of having accidents inside the home. **(5 marks)**

_____

_____

_____

_____

_____

_____

_____

_____

_____

Road accidents involving children

Country	Fatal	Serious	Slight	All severities
England	100	2,295	16,808	19,203
Scotland	20	277	1,392	1,689
Wales	4	111	989	1,104
N. Ireland	7	94	851	952
Great Britain	124	2,638	19,189	21,996
UK (GB+NI)	131	2,777	20,040	22,948

Source: Child Accident Prevention Trust, 2009

5. According to the table above, how many road accidents involving children were there in the UK in 2009? **(1 mark)**

_____

6. Which country in the UK had the lowest number of fatal road accidents involving children in 2009? **(1 mark)**

_____

7. Give _three_ reasons why young children are at risk of being involved in road accidents. **(3 marks)**

i) _____

_____

ii) _____

_____

iii) _____

_____

Heather has twin boys, aged 18 months.
She is very safety conscious and encourages
her friends and relatives who wish to buy
toys or other presents for the twins, to buy
items that include a safety guarantee.

8. What kind of child safety seat should Heather's parents buy for their grandsons so that the boys can travel safely in their car? **(2 marks)**

_____

_____

_____

_____

_____

_____

9. How can Heather's parents ensure that the toys they buy for their grandsons meet the UK minimum safety standards? **(3 marks)**

_____

_____

_____

_____

_____

_____

It is a good idea for parents and other adults who care for children
to have some understanding of simple first aid procedures and to
keep a first aid box handy.

10. Identify _four_ items that should be included in a basic first aid box. **(4 marks)**

i) _____

_____

ii) _____

_____

iii) _____

_____

iv) _____

_____

11. Complete the chart below about the basic treatment that should be provided in these common first aid situations when children are involved. **(6 marks)**

First aid situation	Treatment
Nose bleed	
Choking	
Poisoning	

2) Pregnancy

This chapter covers the following topics:

2.1   Reproduction

2.2   Pre-conceptual care

2.3   Pregnancy

2.4   Preparation for the birth

2.5   Labour and birth

2.6   Newborn baby

2.7   Postnatal care

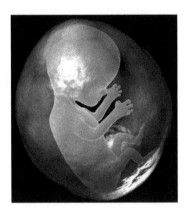

Before you complete the questions in this chapter, begin any controlled assessment tasks, or sit any exam questions related to *Pregnancy*, you will need to have learned about:

▶ the biological processes of reproduction and conception

▶ the growth and development of the embryo and foetus

▶ the importance of pre-conceptual health and care

▶ health in pregnancy and the range of checks and tests that are available as part of antenatal care

▶ the role of different health professionals during pregnancy, birth and the postnatal period

▶ different methods of contraception

▶ the process of labour and birth, including choices for pain relief

▶ the appearance and needs of a newborn baby, including the special needs of premature babies

▶ the postnatal period, including help and support available for new parents.

The questions and activities that follow provide you with an opportunity to develop your knowledge and assess your understanding of the range of topics that are part of this chapter.

Topic 2.1 Reproduction

The main issues covered in this topic include:

▶ the structure and function of the male and female reproductive systems

▶ the process of conception for single and multiple babies

▶ the growth and development of the baby in the uterus (womb).

Refer to the work you have completed in class or to your course textbook if you are unsure about any of the topics covered by these questions, or if you need to remind yourself of the main points.

Questions and activities

1. a) Label the diagram of the male reproductive system from A–J in the spaces provided. **(5 marks)**

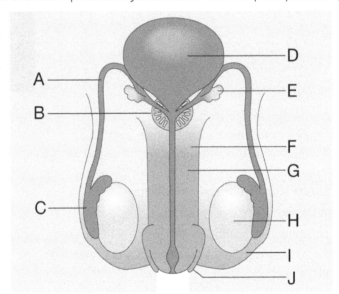

A: _____ F: _____

B: _____ G: _____

C: _____ H: _____

D: _____ I: _____

E: _____ J: _____

b) Complete this table. **(3 marks)**

Sperm are produced in the:	
The male sex hormone is called:	
The mixture of sperm and seminal fluid is called:	

2. a) Label the diagram of the female reproductive system from A–E in the spaces provided. **(5 marks)**

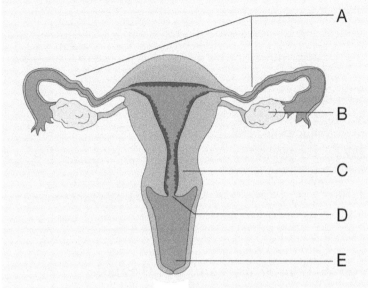

A: _____

B: _____

C: _____

D: _____

E: _____

b) Complete this table. **(3 marks)**

The process of ova (eggs) being released from the ovaries is called:	
The female menstrual cycle lasts for approximately:	
The two female sex hormones are called:	

3. Describe the process of fertilisation. **(6 marks)**

_____

_____

_____

_____

_____

_____

_____

_____

_____

4. Explain the term 'implantation'. **(2 marks)**

_____

_____

_____

> The male sex chromosome is XY and sperm cells can carry either X or Y chromosomes. The female sex chromosome is XX and egg cells will always carry X chromosomes.

5. If a female egg cell is fertilised by a Y sperm cell, what sex will the baby be? **(1 mark)**

_____

6. Describe how non-identical (binovular) twins are conceived. **(3 marks)**

_____

_____

_____

_____

7. Identify _three_ characteristics of non-identical (binovular) twins. **(3 marks)**

i) _____

ii) _____

iii) _____

8. Gemma is an identical (uniovular) twin. Which of these statements is true about her? Tick the correct options. **(3 marks maximum)**

	True
She has the same blood group as her twin.	
She is not the same sex as her twin.	
She looks exactly like her twin.	
She has the same genes as her twin.	

9. Label the diagram from A–H in the spaces provided. **(8 marks)**

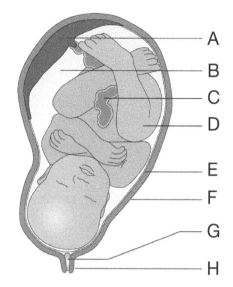

A: _____

B: _____

C: _____

D: _____

E: _____

F: _____

G: _____

H: _____

10. Describe the main functions of the placenta. **(3 marks)**

_____

_____

_____

_____

_____

_____

_____

Topic 2.2 Pre-conceptual care

The main issues covered in this topic are:

▶ the importance of pre-conceptual health and care

▶ different methods of contraception

▶ some of the causes and treatments for infertility.

Refer to the work you have completed in class or to your course textbook if you are unsure about any of the topics covered by these questions, or if you need to remind yourself of the main points.

Questions and activities

1. Complete the table below by providing *two* advantages and *two* disadvantages for each method of contraception. **(12 marks)**

Method of contraception	Advantages	Disadvantages
Male condom	i) _____ _____ ii) _____ _____	i) _____ _____ ii) _____ _____
Intrauterine device (IUD)	i) _____ _____ ii) _____ _____	i) _____ _____ ii) _____ _____
Male sterilisation (vasectomy)	i) _____ _____ ii) _____ _____	i) _____ _____ ii) _____ _____

2. Identify *two* barrier methods of contraception. **(2 marks)**

i) _____

ii) _____

3. Describe how the combined contraceptive pill works as a method of contraception. **(2 marks)**

_____

_____

_____

_____

4. For each of the following examples, describe *two* methods of contraception that would be suitable. Give reasons for your answer.

   a) Ed and Penny have been married for 15 years and have three children aged 5, 11 and 13 years. They do not want more children. **(4 marks)**

      i) _____

         _____

         _____

      ii) _____

         _____

         _____

   b) Parveen and Abdul have been married for two years and would like to have children eventually. **(4 marks)**

      i) _____

         _____

         _____

      ii) _____

         _____

         _____

   c) Sharon is 25 and divorced with two children aged 2 and 4 years. Recently, she started going out with Brian. **(4 marks)**

      i) _____

         _____

         _____

      ii) _____

         _____

         _____

5. Explain how natural family planning works as a method of contraception. **(4 marks)**

_____

_____

_____

_____

_____

_____

6. The combined contraceptive pill contains which *two* hormones? **(2 marks)**

    i) _____

    ii) _____

Tracey is 18 and has been going out with Kevin for six months. Kevin always uses a condom when they have sexual intercourse.

7. Explain why using a condom is an effective method of contraception for Tracey and Kevin. **(2 marks)**

    _____

    _____

    _____

    _____

8. Identify two problems that might occur when Tracey and Kevin are using a condom. **(2 marks)**

    i) _____

    ii) _____

9. Describe what Tracey should do if she ever needs emergency contraception. **(3 marks)**

    _____

    _____

    _____

    _____

10. Explain the term 'contraception' and describe *four* factors that might influence a couple's choice of contraception. **(10 marks)**

    Contraception: _____

    _____

    _____

    i) _____

    _____

    ii) _____

    _____

    iii) _____

    _____

    iv) _____

    _____

Several factors can influence the development of the foetus in the uterus.

11. Complete the following table. **(5 marks)**

Factor	Influence on the foetus
Smoking during pregnancy	
Drinking excessive amounts of alcohol during pregnancy	
Rubella (German measles) virus during pregnancy	
Drugs taken during pregnancy	
Toxoplasmosis during pregnancy	

12. Explain the term 'genetic counselling'. **(4 marks)**

_____

_____

_____

_____

_____

_____

_____

_____

13. Identify two reasons why a couple might decide to have genetic counselling as part of their pre-conceptual health care. **(2 marks)**

i) _____

_____

ii) _____

_____

_____

> Natalie and Simon have been married for six years. They have been trying to conceive a baby for the past five years, but have been unsuccessful so far.

14. Identify *three* possible reasons why Natalie and Simon may have fertility problems. **(3 marks)**

    i) _____

    ii) _____

    iii) _____

15. Explain *two* infertility treatment options that might be available for Natalie and Simon. **(6 marks)**

    i) _____

    ii) _____

16. Identify *two* facts that Natalie and Simon should be aware of about infertility treatment. **(2 marks)**

    i) _____

    ii) _____

Topic 2.3 Pregnancy

The main issues covered in this topic include:

▶ the importance of health during pregnancy

▶ routine antenatal checks and specialised tests

▶ the roles of different health professionals involved in antenatal care.

Refer to the work you have completed in class or to your course textbook if you are unsure about any of the topics covered by these questions, or if you need to remind yourself of the main points.

Questions and activities

> Jane is 28 weeks pregnant. Her general health is good and she sees her midwife regularly. She is working part time as a teaching assistant and her husband is in full-time employment.

1. Describe the routine antenatal checks that will be carried out every time Jane sees her midwife. **(8 marks)**

    _____

    _____

    _____

    _____

    _____

    _____

    _____

    _____

2. Explain *two* specialised tests that may be offered to Jane as part of her antenatal care. **(6 marks)**

   i) _____

   _____

   _____

   ii) _____

   _____

   _____

3. Identify *three* facts about Jane's foetus at this stage of her pregnancy. **(3 marks)**

   i) _____

   ii) _____

   iii) _____

4. Give *two* examples of advice that Jane's midwife may suggest at this stage of her pregnancy. **(4 marks)**

   i) _____

   _____

   ii) _____

   _____

   _____

5. Describe how Jane's husband can support her during her pregnancy. **(4 marks)**

   _____

   _____

   _____

   _____

   _____

6. Identify *four* topics that may be included in parenting classes. **(4 marks)**

   i) _____

   ii) _____

   iii) _____

   iv) _____

7. Describe the roles of the following health professionals in supporting pregnant women and their partners. **(6 marks)**

   a) Midwife: _____

   _____

   _____

   b) Health visitor: _____

   _____

   _____

   c) Obstetrician: _____

   _____

   _____

8. Identify two symptoms of pre-eclampsia. **(2 marks)**

   i) _____

   ii) _____

9. Describe one of the tests that can be used to detect Down's syndrome during pregnancy. **(4 marks)**

   _____

   _____

   _____

   _____

   _____

   _____

10. Explain the term 'ectopic pregnancy'. **(3 marks)**

   _____

   _____

   _____

11. Identify two reasons why a miscarriage may occur. **(2 marks)**

   i) _____

   _____

   ii) _____

   _____

Topic 2.4 Preparation for the birth

The main issues covered in this topic include:

▶ the choices available for the birth of the baby

▶ the support available for new parents

▶ parenting classes and the importance of the father or partner.

Refer to the work you have completed in class or to your course textbook if you are unsure about any of the topics covered by these questions, or if you need to remind yourself of the main points.

Questions and activities

> Jessica is 40 weeks pregnant and is anxious and excited about the birth of her first child. She and her partner Rikki have developed a birth plan with the midwife and Rikki would like to be present during the labour and delivery.

1. Explain *two* factors that Jessica and Rikki may have considered as part of their birth plan. **(4 marks)**

   i) _____

   ii) _____

2. Identify *four* items of information that might be recorded in Jessica's hand-held notes. **(4 marks)**

   i) _____

   ii) _____

   iii) _____

   iv) _____

3. Explain why it is important to record information in held-held notes during pregnancy. **(4 marks)**

   _____

   _____

   _____

   _____

   _____

   _____

   _____

4. Describe *four* benefits that Jessica and Rikki might gain from attending parenting classes. **(4 marks)**

   i) _____

   ii) _____

   iii) _____

   iv) _____

Topic 2.5 Labour and birth

The main issues covered in this topic include:

▶ the stages of labour and the process of birth

▶ the range of pain relief available during labour

▶ complications that can arise during labour and birth.

You should refer to the work you have completed in class or to your course textbook if you are unsure about any of the topics covered by these questions, or to remind yourself of the main points.

Questions and activities

1. Identify *three* signs that could indicate the onset of labour. **(3 marks)**

   i) _____

   _____

   ii) _____

   _____

   iii) _____

   _____

2. Describe the *three* stages of labour that a woman who is giving birth will experience. **(10 marks)**

   i) _____

   _____

   _____

   _____

   ii) _____

   _____

   _____

   _____

   iii) _____

   _____

   _____

   _____

Uschma has decided that she would like to have an epidural anaesthetic for the birth of her child.

3. Describe *two* other methods of pain relief that Uschma could choose to use during labour. **(8 marks)**

i) _____

_____

_____

_____

ii) _____

_____

_____

_____

4. Identify two reasons why labour may be artificially induced. **(2 marks)**

i) _____

_____

ii) _____

_____

5. Arrange statements A to G about the second stage of labour in the correct order. **(7 marks)**

A   The baby's head becomes visible.   _____

B   The cervix is fully dilated.   _____

C   The umbilical cord is clamped and cut.   _____

D   The mother pushes with each contraction.   _____

E   The baby is born.   _____

F   Mucous is cleared from the baby's nose and mouth.   _____

G   The baby is a separate person.   _____

6. Explain how the process of attachment (bonding) can be encouraged immediately after the birth. **(4 marks)**

_____

_____

_____

_____

_____

_____

7. Describe two situations when a Caesarean section may be performed. **(4 marks)**

i) _____

_____

ii) _____

_____

8. Describe the role of the father or partner during labour and birth. **(4 marks)**

_____

_____

_____

_____

_____

_____

Topic 2.6   Newborn baby

The main issues covered in this topic include:

▶ the appearance and abilities of a newborn baby

▶ the baby's need for love, food, warmth, sleep and protection

▶ the routine checks carried out on newborn babies

▶ the special care of premature and low birth weight babies

▶ reducing the risk of cot death.

Refer to the work you have completed in class or to your course textbook if you are unsure about any of the topics covered by these questions, or if you need to remind yourself of the main points.

Questions and activities

All newborn babies are examined at birth to make sure there are no abnormalities.

1. Complete the table below to describe the characteristics of a newborn baby. **(6 marks)**

Characteristic	Description
Fontanelle	
Vernix	
Startle reflex	

2. Describe *two* abnormalities that may be detected following a routine examination of a newborn baby.
   (4 marks)

   i) _____

   _____

   ii) _____

   _____

3. What is the average birth weight of a newborn baby? **(1 mark)**

   _____

4. Identify *two* conditions that are checked for by a routine blood test around six days after a baby is born.
   (2 marks)

   i) _____

   ii) _____

5. Describe *three* basic needs of all newborn babies. **(6 marks)**

   i) _____

   _____

   ii) _____

   _____

   iii) _____

   _____

Julia and Garry's son Chris is 5 weeks old. He is fully breastfed, gaining weight normally and seems very content. Julia takes Chris out each day, usually to the local park or to a parent group at the local health centre. Garry plays with Chris every evening. After being bathed, Chris is put to bed at around 7 pm and wakes for breastfeeds during the night.

6. Explain *three* ways that Julia and Garry can make sure they are meeting Chris' basic needs. **(6 marks)**

   i) _____

   _____

   _____

   ii) _____

   _____

   _____

   iii) _____

   _____

   _____

7. Explain the term 'cot death' and describe *four* factors that can reduce the risk of cot death. **(10 marks)**

_____

_____

_____

_____

_____

_____

_____

_____

_____

_____

Ria gave birth to a boy during the 35th week of pregnancy. The birth was normal and her son weighed 2.2 kg. He is now in an incubator in the Special Care Baby Unit and Ria is in the postnatal ward at the same hospital.

8. Describe *two* reasons why Ria's baby could have been born prematurely. **(4 marks)**

i) _____

_____

ii) _____

_____

9. Identify *two* problems that Ria's baby might experience in the first few days of life. **(2 marks)**

i) _____

_____

ii) _____

_____

10. Explain some of the difficulties that Ria might experience in caring for her premature baby in the first few weeks. **(6 marks)**

_____

_____

_____

_____

_____

_____

_____

_____

_____

_____

Topic 2.7 Postnatal care

The main issues covered in this topic include:

▶ the support available for families with a new baby

▶ the importance of postnatal check-ups for both mother and baby

▶ the importance of good nutrition in the postnatal period.

Refer to the work you have completed in class or to your course textbook if you are unsure about any of the topics covered by these questions, or if you need to remind yourself of the main points.

Questions and activities

Angela gave birth to Sam 2 weeks ago. Sam was born normally and weighed 3.2 kg. Angela is breastfeeding Sam and her midwife is being supportive of this.

1. Identify two physical changes and two emotional changes that Angela may be experiencing at this stage of her postnatal period. **(4 marks)**

Physical	Emotional
i)	i)
ii)	ii)

2. Describe *three* key items of advice that Angela's midwife might discuss with her. **(6 marks)**

    i) _____

    _____

    ii) _____

    _____

    iii) _____

    _____

3. Explain why it is important for Angela to eat healthily at this stage of her postnatal period. **(4 marks)**

    _____

    _____

    _____

    _____

    _____

4. Identify *three* foods that would be good dietary sources of iron for Angela. **(3 marks)**

    i) _____

    ii) _____

    iii) _____

5. Describe how Angela can promote her attachment relationship with Sam at this stage. **(3 marks)**

    _____

    _____

    _____

6. Explain why attachment is so important in the early stages of a baby's life. **(3 marks)**

    _____

    _____

    _____

    _____

7. Describe how Angela's husband could support her during this stage of her postnatal period. **(3 marks)**

    _____

    _____

    _____

When Sam is 6 weeks old, Angela takes him to the baby clinic for a check-up by the health visitor.

8. Describe two checks that the health visitor might carry out on Sam. **(4 marks)**

i) _____

_____

ii) _____

_____

9. Give examples of two questions that the health visitor might ask Angela. **(4 marks)**

a) About herself: i) _____

ii) _____

b) About Sam: i) _____

ii) _____

10. Explain the term 'postnatal depression'. **(4 marks)**

_____

_____

_____

_____

_____

3 Diet, health and care of the child

This chapter covers the following topics:

3.1   Nutrition and healthy eating

3.2   Feeding babies and young children

3.3   Food-related problems

3.4   Childcare

3.5   Child health

Before you complete the questions in this chapter, begin any controlled assessment tasks, or sit any exam questions related to *Diet, health and care of the child*, you will need to have learned about:

▶ that babies and young children have a range of nutritional needs

▶ the function and sources of the major nutrients in a child's diet

▶ the arguments for and against breast and bottle feeding and approaches to weaning

▶ the importance of healthy eating and the links between poor diet and illness

▶ how immunity to disease and infection can be acquired

▶ how to prevent, recognise and manage childhood illness

▶ the needs of sick children.

The questions and activities that follow provide you with an opportunity to develop your knowledge and assess your understanding of the topics, as listed above.

Topic 3.1 Nutrition and healthy eating

The main issues covered in this topic are:

▶ the importance of healthy eating for young children

▶ the major nutrients and main food groups

▶ how to encourage healthy eating habits in young children.

Refer to the work you have completed in class or to your course textbook if you are unsure about any of the topics covered by these questions, or if you need to remind yourself of the main points.

Questions and activities

1. Complete the following table about food, the main nutrients and their function in the body.
   (10 marks maximum)

Nutrient	Function in the body	Example foods
Protein		meat, fish, milk, cheese, eggs, soya, beans, pulses
Carbohydrate (starches and sugars)	to provide energy	
	to provide warmth and energy	butter, cream, cheese, eggs, olive oil, nuts
Vitamin: A	healthy skin and eyes	
Vitamin B group		wholegrain cereals and bread
Vitamin C	protection against infection	
Vitamin D		oily fish, eggs, natural sunlight on the skin
Iron	healthy red blood cells	
	strong bones and teeth	milk, cheese, yoghurt, nuts, green vegetables
Fibre		fruit, vegetables, wholegrain cereals and bread

2. Explain how to encourage young children to eat healthily. **(6 marks)**

_____
_____
_____
_____
_____
_____

3. Describe *three* factors that can influence a child's diet. **(6 marks)**

_____

_____

_____

_____

_____

_____

4. Plan a healthy, balanced meal, including drinks, for the following children.

In each case, list all the nutrients you have included and give reasons for your choices.

a) Lunch for Jack, aged 5 years, who is allergic to wheat flour. **(4 marks)**

_____

_____

_____

_____

_____

_____

b) Dinner for Liad, aged 3 years, who is Jewish. **(4 marks)**

_____

_____

_____

_____

_____

_____

c) Breakfast for Lucy, aged 18 months, whose parents want her to be vegan. **(4 marks)**

_____

_____

_____

_____

_____

_____

Topic 3.2 Feeding babies and young children

The main issues covered in this topic are:

▶ the advantages of both breastfeeding and bottle feeding

▶ the differences between breast milk and formula milk

▶ how to make up a bottle feed and sterilise feeding equipment

▶ the process of weaning babies onto solid food.

Refer to the work you have completed in class or to your course textbook if you are unsure about any of the topics covered by these questions, or if you need to remind yourself of the main points.

Questions and activities

> Mary is currently on maternity leave from her full-time job as a teacher. She is breastfeeding her baby, Emma, who is now 10 days old. The midwife has been visiting Mary every day and has been advising her about breastfeeding.

1. Give *three* examples of advice that the midwife may give to Mary about breastfeeding. **(3 marks)**

   i) _____

   ii) _____

   iii) _____

2. Identify *four* advantages of breastfeeding for baby Emma. **(4 marks)**

   i) _____

   ii) _____

   iii) _____

   iv) _____

3. Describe *two* disadvantages that Mary might consider about breastfeeding Emma. **(4 marks)**

   i) _____

   _____

   ii) _____

   _____

4. Explain the term 'colostrum' and identify two of the characteristics. **(3 marks)**

   _____

   _____

   _____

5. Arrange statements A to J about making up bottle feeds, in the correct order. **(10 marks)**

   A   Carefully place the teat and cap onto the bottle and shake gently.

   B   Pour the correct amount of cooled boiled water into the feeding bottle.

   C   Check the temperature of the milk by shaking a few drops onto the inside of your wrist; it should feel lukewarm, not hot.

   D   Clean the surface where the feed will be prepared.

   E   Cool the milk quickly by holding the bottle under cold running water or placing the bottle in a container of cold water.

   F   Measure the exact amount of milk powder as recommended on the instructions using the scoop provided. Add into the feeding bottle.

   G   Make sure all feeding equipment is properly sterilised.

   H   Boil the water and leave it to cool.

   I   Wash your hands thoroughly.

   J   Check that the amount of water is at the correct measure on the side of the bottle.

Correct order: _____

6. Identify *three* ways to sterilise feeding equipment. **(3 marks)**

   i) _____

   ii) _____

   iii) _____

7. Explain why it is important to sterilise the feeding equipment for babies. **(3 marks)**

_____

_____

_____

_____

> Jamie is 10 weeks old and has been admitted to hospital with gastroenteritis.

8. Describe the main symptoms of gastroenteritis. **(4 marks)**

_____

_____

_____

_____

_____

9. Identify *two* factors that could have caused Jamie's gastroenteritis. **(2 marks)**

   i) _____

   ii) _____

10. Describe the main dangers of gastroenteritis in young babies. **(3 marks)**

_____

_____

_____

_____

_____

11. What advice would you give to Jamie's parents about preventing gastroenteritis in the future? **(3 marks)**

_____

_____

_____

_____

_____

12. It is important to follow safe practice when bottle feeding a baby. Identify _four_ factors about safe bottle feeding practice. **(4 marks)**

i) _____

_____

ii) _____

_____

iii) _____

_____

iv) _____

_____

13. Complete the table below about the process of weaning (starting on solid foods). **(16 marks maximum)**

Stage of weaning and age	Consistency of food	Suitable examples
Stage:_____ Age: _____	pureed	baby rice mixed with breast or bottle milk, carrot, banana, lentils
Second About 6–9 months	_____	potato, cooked apple, dhal, yoghurt, carrot sticks, pitta bread, rusks
Stage:_____ Age: _____	chopped	_____ _____ _____ _____ _____

Omar is 7 months old and has gradually been enjoying some solid food for the past 3 weeks. He still has a breastfeed first thing in the morning and before he goes to bed at night.

14. What stage of weaning has Omar reached? **(1 mark)**

_____

15. Identify *four* suitable foods for Omar at this stage of his weaning process. **(4 marks)**

i) _____

ii) _____

iii) _____

iv) _____

16. Explain the advice that should be given to Omar's parents about continuing to wean Omar over the next few months. **(8 marks)**

_____

_____

_____

_____

_____

_____

_____

_____

_____

_____

_____

Topic 3.3 Food-related problems

The main issues covered in this topic are:

▶ the links between diet and health issues for young children

▶ food allergies and intolerances in young children

▶ food-related problems for young children.

You should refer to the work you have completed in class or to your course textbook if you are unsure about any of the topics covered by these questions or to remind yourself of the main points.

Questions and activities

1. Identify two diet-related conditions that can affect young children. **(2 marks)**

i) _____

ii) _____

2. Explain the term 'food intolerance' and identify *three* foods that can cause this in young children. **(6 marks)**

_____

_____

_____

_____

_____

_____

Helena is 18 months old and has recently begun to refuse food at mealtimes. Her mother has tried a variety of foods, but Helena has refused them all. Mealtimes have become very difficult and frustrating for them both.

3. Explain the reasons why Helena may be refusing food at mealtimes. **(3 marks)**

_____

_____

_____

4. Describe the advice you might give to Helena's mother to help improve this situation. **(4 marks)**

_____

_____

_____

_____

5. Explain the term 'attention deficit hyperactivity syndrome (ADHD)' and identify *two* foods that are commonly associated with this condition in children. **(4 marks)**

_____

_____

_____

_____

_____

6. Explain how tooth decay happens and identify *two* foods that are commonly associated with this condition in children. **(6 marks)**

_____

_____

_____

_____

_____

_____

Topic 3.4 Childcare

The main issues covered in this topic are:

▶ the importance of hygiene in caring for babies and young children

▶ bathing babies and changing nappies

▶ suitable clothing and footwear for babies and children.

You should refer to the work you have completed in class or to your course textbook if you are unsure about any of the topics covered by these questions or to remind yourself of the main points.

Questions and activities

1. Explain why cleanliness is important for the physical health and development of babies and young children.
(2 marks)

_____

_____

_____

_____

2. Explain what 'topping and tailing' involves. **(1 mark)**

_____

_____

_____

3. Describe a safe, effective technique for bathing a baby. Outline the tasks that need to be done to prepare the bath, describe a safe bathing technique and explain how the baby should be dried after being bathed.
(8 marks)

_____

_____

_____

_____

_____

_____

_____

_____

_____

_____

_____

_____

Parents should consider a range of factors when choosing clothes and footwear for their children. Appropriate clothing and footwear are needed for different conditions and occasions.

4. Identify *four* factors that parents should consider when choosing clothing or footwear for their children. **(4 marks)**

   i) _____

   ii) _____

   iii) _____

   iv) _____

5. If you had to give a parent advice on choosing suitable nightwear for a 2-year-old child, what *three* points would you tell them? **(3 marks)**

   i) _____

   ii) _____

   iii) _____

6. Why should a young child have his or her feet measured regularly? **(3 marks)**

   _____

   _____

   _____

   _____

7. Identify *three* factors that parents should take into account when choosing shoes for their children. **(3 marks)**

   i) _____

   ii) _____

   iii) _____

8. Describe *three* ways that good footwear can promote a young child's physical health and development. **(3 marks)**

   i) _____

   _____

   ii) _____

   _____

   iii) _____

   _____

Topic 3.5 Child health

The main issues covered in this topic are:

▶ how infection is caused and how it can spread

▶ the common infectious diseases of childhood

▶ how children develop immunity to disease

▶ how to recognise childhood illness

▶ how to care for a sick child and when to seek medical help

▶ how to prepare a child for a stay in hospital.

Refer to the work you have completed in class or to your course textbook if you are unsure about any of the topics covered by these questions, or if you need to remind yourself of the main points.

Questions and activities

1. Identify *five* factors that help to keep young children healthy. **(5 marks)**

   i) _____

   ii) _____

   iii) _____

   iv) _____

   v) _____

2. Describe the causes and symptoms of the following childhood conditions. **(12 marks maximum)**

   a) Asthma: _____

   _____

   _____

   b) Chicken pox: _____

   _____

   _____

   c) Meningitis: _____

   _____

   _____

3. Identify *five* signs of illness in a child. **(5 marks)**

   i) _____

   ii) _____

   iii) _____

   iv) _____

   v) _____

4. Explain how infection can be spread among young children in a nursery classroom. **(6 marks)**

_____
_____
_____
_____
_____
_____
_____
_____

5. Explain the term 'immunity' and describe two ways young children can develop immunity to diseases.
   (6 marks)

_____
_____
_____
_____
_____
_____
_____
_____

6. Complete the following table about routine childhood immunisations and the ages at which they are given.
   (6 marks)

Age given	Immunisation against (vaccine given)
2 months	Diphtheria, tetanus, pertussis (whooping cough) (**DTaP**) polio (**IPV**) and Haemophilus influenzae type b (**Hib**), which can cause meningitis) Pneumococcal infection (**PCV**)
_____	Diphtheria, tetanus, pertussis (whooping cough) (**DTaP**) polio (**IPV**) and Haemophilus influenzae type b (**Hib**) Meningitis C (**Men C**)
_____	Diphtheria, tetanus, pertussis (whooping cough) (**DTaP**) polio (**IPV**) and Haemophilus influenzae type b (**Hib**) Meningitis C (**Men C**) Pneumococcal infection (**PCV**)
Around 12 months	_____
_____	Measles, mumps and rubella (**MMR**) Pneumococcal infection (**PCV**)
3 years and 4 months (or soon after)	Diphtheria, tetanus, pertussis (whooping cough) (**DTaP**) and polio (**IPV**) _____

Jamil is 4 years old and is due to go into hospital next week for some investigations, including blood tests and X-rays. He will need to stay in hospital overnight, but will not be having an operation or a general anaesthetic. Jamil's mum will go with him and is planning to stay at the hospital until Jamil is ready to come home.

7. Explain how Jamil's mum could help to prepare him for going into hospital. **(8 marks)**

_____

_____

_____

_____

_____

_____

_____

_____

_____

8. Describe how Jamil might be affected by going into hospital. **(6 marks)**

_____

_____

_____

_____

_____

_____

_____

_____

9. Identify *four* toys or play activities that might help Jamil with this experience. Give reasons for your answers. **(8 marks)**

i) _____

_____

ii) _____

_____

iii) _____

_____

iv) _____

_____

10. Describe *two* ways to take a child's temperature. **(4 marks)**

    i) _____
    _____
    _____

    ii) _____
    _____
    _____

11. Explain the term 'febrile convulsion' and describe *three* factors that can help to prevent this. **(5 marks)**

    _____
    _____
    _____
    _____
    _____
    _____
    _____
    _____
    _____

12. Identify *four* important symptoms in a sick child, which indicate that medical help is needed. **(4 marks)**

    i) _____
    ii) _____
    iii) _____
    iv) _____

4) Development of the child

This chapter covers the following topics:

4.1   Growth and development

4.2   Physical development

4.3   Intellectual and language development

4.4   Social and emotional development

4.5   Learning and play

Before you complete the questions in this chapter, begin any controlled assessment tasks, or sit any exam questions related to *Development of the child*, you will need to have learned about:

▶ the factors influencing growth and development in children from birth to 5

▶ the range of normal physical, intellectual, emotional and social development in children from birth to 5

▶ the importance of play for young children

▶ the different ways that children learn through play.

The questions and activities that follow provide you with an opportunity to develop your knowledge and assess your understanding of the range of topics, as listed above.

Topic 4.1 Growth and development

The main issues covered in this topic include:

▶ the difference between growth and development

▶ the factors that can influence growth and development from birth to 5 years

▶ how growth and development are monitored in the first 5 years of life.

Refer to the work you have completed in class or to your course textbook if you are unsure about any of the topics covered by these questions, or if you need to remind yourself of the main points.

Questions and activities

1. Explain the difference between the following terms. **(4 marks)**

   a) Growth: _____

   _____

   b) Development: _____

   _____

> Annika is an experienced childminder. She has been asked to make a presentation to a group of students on an introductory childcare course. Annika's presentation will focus on promoting the physical development of young children.

2. One of the students asks Annika why babies and toddlers need so much sleep. What would you say if you were in Annika's position? **(3 marks)**

   _____

   _____

   _____

   _____

3. Another student asks Annika about centile charts. She wants to know what they are and how they are used. What would you say if you were in Annika's position? **(4 marks)**

   _____

   _____

   _____

   _____

   _____

   _____

4. Identify *five* factors that can promote the development of children. **(5 marks)**

i) _____

ii) _____

iii) _____

iv) _____

v) _____

5. Explain the importance of the following conditions for children's development. **(6 marks)**

a) Housing environment: _____

_____

_____

b) Exercise: _____

_____

_____

Topic 4.2 Physical development

The main issues covered in this topic are:

▶ the normal stages of physical development

▶ some of the factors that can influence physical development

▶ some of the ways to encourage children's physical development
   at different stages.

Refer to the work you have completed in class or to your course textbook if you
are unsure about any of the topics covered by these questions, or if you need to
remind yourself of the main points.

Questions and activities

Physical development
includes the
development of gross
and fine motor skills and
sensory abilities.

1. Explain the meaning of the following terms. **(2 marks)**

a) Gross motor skills: _____

_____

a) Fine motor skills: _____

_____

2. Complete the table on the next page, which lists milestones of physical development. Give two examples of
   gross or fine motor skills at each stage, as indicated. **(12 marks)**

Age	Gross motor skills	Fine motor skills
3 months	i) _____ ii) _____	Plays with hands Holds an object for a short time)
6 months	Sits with some support Rolls over	i) _____ ii) _____
1 year	i) _____ ii) _____	Points with index finger Claps hands together
18 months	i) _____ ii) _____	Feeds self with a spoon Builds a tower of three blocks
2–3 years	Throws and kicks a ball Runs Walks upstairs	i) _____ ii) _____
5 years	i) _____ ii) _____	Uses a knife and fork Fastens and unfastens buttons

Emily is 18 months old. She can walk sturdily by herself and enjoys going up stairs, carefully lifting both feet onto each step as she goes. She can feed herself with a spoon and enjoys crayoning with chunky wax crayons.

3. Describe two ways to encourage Emily's gross motor skills. **(4 marks)**

   i) _____

   _____

   _____

   ii) _____

   _____

   _____

4. Describe two ways to encourage Emily's fine motor skills. **(4 marks)**

   i) _____

   _____

   _____

   ii) _____

   _____

   _____

5. Explain why it is important for Emily to play outside to develop her physical skills. **(5 marks)**

_____

_____

_____

_____

_____

_____

_____

6. Give examples of _three_ activities that would encourage the fine motor skills of a 4-year-old child. Give reasons for your answers. **(6 marks)**

_____

_____

_____

_____

_____

_____

_____

_____

7. Give examples of _three_ activities that would encourage the vision and hearing of a 3-month-old baby. Give reasons for your answers. **(6 marks)**

_____

_____

_____

_____

_____

_____

_____

8. Identify two signs, which could indicate that a baby is teething. **(2 marks)**

_____

_____

_____

9. Explain why it is important for parents to encourage good dental health in young children and describe some of the ways they can do this. **(8 marks)**

_____

_____

_____

_____

_____

_____

_____

_____

Topic 4.3 Intellectual and language development

The main issues covered in this topic are:

▶ the normal stages of intellectual and language development from birth to 5

▶ some of the factors that can influence intellectual and language development

▶ some of the ways to encourage children's intellectual and language development at different stages.

Refer to the work you have completed in class or to your course textbook if you are unsure about any of the topics covered by these questions, or if you need to remind yourself of the main points.

Questions and activities

1. Identify _two_ abilities that improve in young children as a result of intellectual development. **(2 marks)**

   i) _____

   ii) _____

2. Describe _three_ ways in which babies explore and learn about their environment in the early weeks and months of life. **(3 marks)**

   i) _____

   _____

   ii) _____

   _____

   iii) _____

   _____

3. Describe *three* conditions or factors that promote children's learning and intellectual development.
   (3 marks)

   i) _____

   _____

   _____

   ii) _____

   _____

   _____

   iii) _____

   _____

   _____

Daniel is 18 months old. His mum is wondering how she can promote his learning
and intellectual development. Her sister, who is a teacher, mentions that nature
and nurture factors play a part in this area of child development.

4. If Daniel's mum were to ask you what 'nature' and 'nurture' factors are, how would you explain this to her?
   (4 marks)

   _____

   _____

   _____

   _____

   _____

   _____

   _____

   _____

5. Describe *two* examples of toys that could be used to stimulate Daniel's learning and intellectual development
   over the next 6 months. **(4 marks)**

   _____

   _____

   _____

   _____

   _____

   _____

   _____

6. Using an example, explain how young children like Daniel learn through imitation. **(4 marks)**

_____

_____

_____

_____

_____

_____

_____

7. How does looking at books and being read stories help a child's intellectual development? **(4 marks)**

_____

_____

_____

_____

_____

8. Complete the table below by giving an example of how each person can help to promote a child's learning and intellectual development. **(4 marks)**

Care role	Example: What can I do to promote early learning?
Parent	
Childminder	
Playgroup worker	
Pre-school teacher	

Yasmin is 9 months old. Her sister Bella is 2 years of age. Her cousin Dean is 4 years old. All three children spend time together but are at different stages of intellectual development.

9. Identify *one* intellectual development norm or 'milestone' that you would expect each child to have reached. **(3 marks)**

a) Yasmin: _____

_____

b) Bella: _____

_____

c) Dean: _____

_____

10. What kind of numeracy skills would you expect Dean to have by the age of 4? **(4 marks)**

_____

_____

_____

_____

11. Identify *three* ways to encourage babies to develop their language skills. **(3 marks)**

i) _____

ii) _____

iii) _____

12. Indicate whether each of these statements is true or false by completing the box next to it with a T (True) or F (False). **(5 marks)**

Statement	True (T)	False (F)
a) Boys' language development tends to be slower than girls'.		
b) A child's language development will improve if the brother or sister speaks for him or her.		
c) Children with hearing impairments may experience slower and more limited language development.		
d) Parents who read stories and sing nursery rhymes to their children help to promote their language development.		
e) Babies and young children learn some language skills by mimicking others.		

Children's language development progresses through a sequence of stages marked by 'milestones' or developmental norms.

13. Describe two examples of language development 'milestones' that babies reach in the first 6 months of their lives. **(4 marks)**

_____

_____

_____

_____

_____

_____

_____

_____

14. Describe two examples of language development 'milestones' that young children are likely to reach before their second birthday. **(4 marks)**

_____

_____

_____

_____

_____

_____

_____

_____

_____

15. At what age would you expect a child to be able to use sentences that describe what she or he can see or feel? **(1 mark)**

_____

_____

16. Outline the reasons why some children learn to speak and understand language more slowly than others. **(6 marks)**

_____

_____

_____

_____

_____

_____

_____

_____

_____

Topic 4.4 Social and emotional development

The main issues covered in this topic are:

▶ the key milestones of social and emotional development during early childhood

▶ the factors that can influence social and emotional development during infancy and early childhood

▶ the importance of attachment and bonding for emotional development

▶ the links between social development and children's behaviour.

Refer to the work you have completed in class or to your course textbook if you are unsure about any of the topics covered by these questions, or if you need to remind yourself of the main points.

Questions and activities

1. What does the term 'bonding' refer to in relation to emotional development? **(2 marks)**

_____

_____

_____

2. Explain why bonding is important for a baby's emotional development. **(2 marks)**

_____

_____

_____

_____

3. What is an 'attachment relationship' and why is it important for emotional development? **(3 marks)**

_____

_____

_____

_____

_____

4. Identify *three* factors that affect the quality of the attachment relationship that develops between a child and his or her parent(s). **(3 marks)**

i) _____

ii) _____

iii) _____

Miriam is 18 months of age. She has become very clingy and cries when she is left in a room without her mum or dad. She is reassured when they return and settles down quickly.

5. Explain why Miriam reacts in the way she does when her parents leave the room. **(3 marks)**

_____

_____

_____

_____

_____

_____

_____

_____

6. Identify *two* ways that Miriam's parents can help her to overcome the worries she has at the moment. **(2 marks)**

i) _____

_____

_____

ii) _____

_____

_____

7. Identify *four* factors that promote the emotional development of babies and young children. **(4 marks)**

i) _____

ii) _____

iii) _____

iv) _____

8. What happens when a child 'regresses'? **(2 marks)**

_____

_____

9. Describe *two* things a child's parent's can do to help her or him to overcome regression problems. **(2 marks)**

i) _____

_____

_____

ii) _____

_____

_____

10. Outline the main ways a child develops emotionally between birth and his or her third birthday. **(10 marks)**

_____

_____

_____

_____

_____

_____

_____

_____

_____

_____

_____

_____

_____

11. What does the term 'socialisation' refer to? **(2 marks)**

_____

_____

_____

Kathryn is 2 years of age. Her mum says, 'Kathryn is very egocentric at the moment. She has tantrums and refuses to share her toys with her older sister'.

12. What does Kathryn's mum mean when she says that Kathryn is 'egocentric'? **(2 marks)**

_____

_____

_____

_____

13. Describe two things that Kathryn's mum could do to help Kathryn develop her social skills and relationships with other children. **(4 marks)**

    i) _____

       _____

    ii) _____

       _____

14. Describe the general pattern of social development and key milestones experienced by children between birth and 3 years of age. **(12 marks)**

_____

_____

_____

_____

_____

_____

_____

_____

_____

_____

_____

_____

_____

_____

_____

_____

Children need good discipline in order to learn acceptable patterns of behaviour.

15. Describe a method of teaching good discipline to young children. **(5 marks)**

_____

_____

_____

_____

_____

16. Explain why children need to learn acceptable patterns of behaviour. **(10 marks)**

_____

_____

_____

_____

_____

_____

_____

_____

> Sean is 3 years old. He has recently started attending nursery, three mornings a week. When he comes home from nursery, Sean becomes aggressive towards his mum. He has started shouting and hitting out at her. Sean's mum isn't sure what she can do about this.

17. Describe two ways in which Sean's mum could respond to his aggressive behaviour when he gets home from nursery. **(2 marks)**

    i) _____

    _____

    ii) _____

    _____

18. Give two reasons why smacking children like Sean for negative behaviour is controversial. **(2 marks)**

    i) _____

    _____

    ii) _____

    _____

Topic 4.5 Learning and play

The main issues covered in this topic are:

▶ how to identify and describe different types of play

▶ how children's play changes as they grow and develop in early childhood

▶ the importance of choosing safe and age-appropriate toys for younger children.

Refer to the work you have completed in class or to your course textbook if you are unsure about any of the topics covered by these questions, or if you need to remind yourself of the main points.

Questions and activities

1. Identify *five* 'early years' settings in which pre-school children can participate in play activities. **(5 marks)**

    i) _____
    ii) _____
    iii) _____
    iv) _____
    v) _____

Rashida has just obtained a part-time job as a nursery assistant. Lizzy, her supervisor, has told her that children play in different ways, depending on their overall stage of development. Lizzy has encouraged Rashida to watch out for the different ways that children play.

2. Identity *four* types of children's play that Rashida might see at the nursery. **(4 marks)**

    i) _____

    _____

    ii) _____

    _____

    iii) _____

    _____

    iv) _____

    _____

3. What happens when children engage in 'parallel play'? **(2 marks)**

    _____

    _____

    _____

    _____

4. Describe *two* ways in which Rashida could use play to promote the learning and development. **(6 marks)**

    i) _____

    _____

    _____

    _____

    _____

    ii) _____

    _____

    _____

    _____

    _____

Rashida has noticed that a couple of children like to use the dressing-up clothes to play a game they call 'mum and dad'. This involves holding hands, looking after a baby doll and pretending to make a meal.

5. What kind of play are the children engaging in? **(1 mark)**

_____

6. What do children learn through games like 'mum and dad'? Describe the different ways in which a child might develop by playing this kind of game. **(5 marks)**

_____

_____

_____

_____

_____

_____

_____

_____

A huge range of toys for babies and children is available in the shops. Choosing children's toys can be fun for parents. However, it is important for them to think about their child's safety and development before buying a toy.

7. Identify *four* safety hazards that parents should look out for when choosing toys for their children. **(4 marks)**

i) _____

ii) _____

iii) _____

iv) _____

8. Complete the table below, identifying developmentally appropriate toys and the abilities they promote for children in each age group identified. **(8 marks)**

Age	Suitable toy	Abilities promoted
a) 6-month-old child		
b) 18-month-old child		
c) 3-year-old child		
d) 5-year-old child		

5) Support for the parent and child

This chapter covers the following topics:

5.1   Types of support for parents and children

5.2   Childcare provision

5.3   Educational provision and the Early Years Foundation Stage (EYFS)

5.4   Support for families of children with special needs

Before you complete the questions in this chapter, begin any controlled assessment tasks, or sit any exam questions related to *Support for the parent and child*, you will need to have learned about:

▶ the range of different forms of childcare provision for parents and children in the UK

▶ the advantages and disadvantages of different types of childcare provision

▶ the main principles of the EYFS curriculum

▶ the care and support available for children with special needs.

The questions and activities that follow provide you with an opportunity to develop your knowledge and assess your understanding of the range of topics, as listed above.

Topic 5.1 Types of support for parents and children

The main issues covered in this topic are:

▶ the main sources and types of support for children and families

▶ how families can access statutory, private and voluntary sector services and support for their children

▶ how families can access support from integrated children's services.

Refer to the work you have completed in class or to your course textbook if you are unsure about any of the topics covered by these questions, or if you need to remind yourself of the main points.

Questions and activities

1. Identify the two organisations that provide most of the statutory care services for children and families.
(2 marks)

   i) _____

   ii) _____

2. Give two examples of statutory services that are provided for children and families. **(2 marks)**

   i) _____

   ii) _____

> Statutory services for children and families are obtained through a referral system.

3. Explain who makes each of the following types of referrals for statutory care services. **(3 marks)**

   i) Self-referral: _____

   ii) Professional referral: _____

   iii) Third-party referral: _____

4. Identify the type of referral being used to obtain statutory services in each of the scenarios below. **(3 marks)**

Scenario	Type of referral
a) Jacqui is worried about a rash that has developed on her baby's arms and legs. She made an appointment for today to see her GP about this.	
b) Becky is a nursery school teacher. She has asked one of her colleagues to carry out a special needs assessment on Andre.	
c) Victoria's mum has phoned a local Sure Start children's centre to put her granddaughter's name down for supported play sessions.	

5. Describe the role of a social worker in a children and families team. **(4 marks)**

_____

_____

_____

_____

_____

_____

6. Describe the role of health visitors in caring for the mother and baby after the birth. **(6 marks)**

_____

_____

_____

_____

_____

_____

_____

_____

7. Identify _three_ sources of financial support that are available from statutory services for children and families. **(3 marks)**

i) _____

_____

ii) _____

_____

iii) _____

_____

Integrated children's services are a new feature of statutory services that have developed since the Children Act (2004).

8. Describe _three_ kinds of services that are offered by integrated children's services in the UK. **(6 marks)**

i) _____

_____

ii) _____

_____

iii) _____

_____

Erin, aged 2, and her brother Charlie, aged 3, attend the Red Balloon Nursery. The nursery is run by a company that specialises in day care for pre-school children. Erin and Charlie's parents pay a weekly fee to the nursery company to enable them to attend.

9. Is the Red Balloon Nursery company a voluntary sector or private sector provider? **(1 mark)**

_____

10. Identify two characteristics of a voluntary sector provider of services for children and families. **(2 marks)**

   i) _____

   ii) _____

11. Identify two characteristics of a private sector provider of services for children and families. **(2 marks)**

   i) _____

   ii) _____

12. Describe two examples of services provided by local voluntary sector organisations for pre-school children and families. **(2 marks)**

   i) _____

   _____

   ii) _____

   _____

13. Use the internet to research one of the large voluntary sector organisations referred to above. Find out about the range of services that they offer, who works for them and how they work in partnership with others. Summarise your findings. **(15 marks)**

_____

_____

_____

_____

_____

_____

_____

_____

_____

_____

_____

14. Identify *four* types of private sector organisation that provide services for pre-school children and families. **(4 marks)**

i) _____

ii) _____

iii) _____

iv) _____

Topic 5.2 Childcare provision

The main issues covered in this topic are:

▶ the reasons why families use childcare provision

▶ different types of childcare provision

▶ the advantages and disadvantages of different types of childcare provision.

Refer to the work you have completed in class or to your course textbook if you are unsure about any of the topics covered by these questions, or if you need to remind yourself of the main points.

Questions and activities

1. Name *four* forms of day care provision available for pre-school children in the UK. **(4 marks)**

i) _____

ii) _____

iii) _____

iv) _____

2. Explain why the demand for day care provision has risen steadily over the last 25 years in the UK. **(4 marks)**

_____

_____

_____

_____

_____

_____

_____

_____

_____

_____

Andrea has twin daughters who are 2½ years old. She works part-time as an accountant, job-sharing with another woman who also has childcare responsibilities. On the three days when she goes to work, Andrea takes her daughters to a local nursery for day care provision from 9 am, until 3.30 pm, when she collects them.

3. Why does Andrea use day care provision for her daughters? **(1 mark)**

_____

_____

4. Explain how job-sharing can be beneficial for working parents. **(2 marks)**

_____

_____

_____

_____

_____

_____

_____

_____

5. Identify *two* other ways in which Andrea's employer could provide her with flexible working arrangements to enable her to combine work and childcare responsibilities. **(2 marks)**

i) _____

_____

_____

ii) _____

_____

_____

Pre-school learning is regulated by the Early Years Foundation Stage (EYFS) curriculum. This framework sets out the child welfare and learning and development standards for children under 5 years of age.

6. Identify *three* areas of early learning that are covered by the EYFS curriculum. **(3 marks)**

i) _____

ii) _____

iii) _____

7. Investigate day care provision in your local area. Summarise your findings by completing the table below. **(8 marks)**

Type of day care	Example of local service	What services are provided for children?
a) Day nursery		
b) Nursery school		
c) Playgroup		
d) Crèche		

8. What role does OFSTED play in relation to day care provision for pre-school children? Carry out some research into this and summarise your findings. **(4 marks)**

_____
_____
_____
_____
_____

Jennifer is a registered childminder. She provides private sector day care for three children in her home.

9. Investigate and describe the role of a childminder. Provide a summary of:

a) the type of services that childminders offer

b) the skills needed to be a childminder

c) the standards of care that childminders have to meet. **(15 marks)**

_____
_____
_____
_____
_____
_____
_____
_____
_____
_____
_____

10. Describe *three* reasons why a child's parents may choose to use a childminder rather than another form of day care provision. **(3 marks)**

i) _____
_____

ii) _____
_____

iii) _____
_____

11. Explain the term 'informal care'. **(2 marks)**

_____
_____
_____
_____
_____
_____

12. Describe *three* forms of informal care that you would expect to be provided for pre-school children in the UK. **(6 marks)**

i) _____
_____
_____
_____

ii) _____
_____
_____
_____

iii) _____
_____
_____
_____

Topic 5.3 Educational provision and the Early Years Foundation Stage (EYFS)

The main issues covered in this topic are:

▶ The main principles of the EYFS

▶ The six areas of learning in the EYFS

▶ The advantages and disadvantages of the EYFS

You should refer to the work you have completed in class or to your course textbook if you are unsure about any of the topics covered by these questions or to remind yourself of the main points.

Questions and activities

> Geraldine is a teacher at Elmers Road, a pre-school nursery for children aged 3 and 4. She has to implement the Early Years Foundation Stage (EYFS) curriculum as part of her work.

1. Explain what the EYFS curriculum is and outline the *four* main themes it contains. **(6 marks)**

_____

_____

_____

_____

_____

_____

_____

_____

_____

_____

2. Identify *three* different areas of early learning that are covered by the EYFS curriculum. **(3 marks)**

i) _____

ii) _____

iii) _____

3. Describe a play activity that Geraldine might plan for the pre-school children in her class, which would help to develop their problem-solving, reasoning and numeracy skills. **(8 marks)**

_____

_____

_____

_____

_____

_____

_____

_____

_____

_____

4. Describe a play activity that Geraldine might plan for the pre-school children in her class, which would help to develop their knowledge and understanding of the world. **(8 marks)**

_____

_____

_____

_____

_____

_____

_____

_____

_____

_____

5. Identify two advantages and two disadvantages of the EYFS curriculum. **(4 marks)**

a) Advantages

i) _____

ii) _____

b) Disadvantages

i) _____

ii) _____

Topic 5.4 Support for families with children with special needs

The main issues covered in this topic are:

▶ the different kinds of special needs

▶ why some children have special needs

▶ caring for a child with special needs in a range of ways.

Refer to the work you have completed in class or to your course textbook if you are unsure about any of the topics covered by these questions, or if you need to remind yourself of the main points.

Questions and activities

1. Name *three* reasons why a child may have special needs. **(3 marks)**

    i) _____

    ii) _____

    iii) _____

2. Describe the effects of foetal alcohol syndrome on a child's physical and intellectual development. **(4 marks)**

    _____

    _____

    _____

    _____

    _____

3. Investigate the condition of Down's syndrome that affects approximately one in every 1000 babies in the UK. Using your findings, describe the kinds of special needs that children with Down's syndrome have. **(5 marks)**

    _____

    _____

    _____

    _____

    _____

    _____

    _____

    _____

    _____

    _____

    _____

A family who has a child with
special needs may require
additional support.

4. Describe the effects a child with special needs could have on other children in the family. **(6 marks)**

_____

_____

_____

_____

_____

_____

_____

_____

5. Identify _three_ ways in which relatives could support and assist a family who have a child with special needs.
   (3 marks)

   i) _____

   _____

   ii) _____

   _____

   iii) _____

   _____

6. Describe _three_ support services that are available to families who are caring for children with special needs.
   (6 marks)

   i) _____

   _____

   _____

   ii) _____

   _____

   _____

   iii) _____

   _____

   _____

Haroon, aged 3, has complex physical and learning disabilities. He normally lives at home with his parents and younger brother in a specially adapted bungalow. Caring for Haroon is tiring and quite stressful for his parents. As a result, they take Haroon to a residential centre for children with special needs for a week-long respite break every 3 months. Haroon is looked after by qualified nursing and Early Years staff for a week while his parents and brother take a holiday or have a break at home.

7. What is respite care? **(1 mark)**

_____

_____

8. Describe the main benefits of respite care. **(4 marks)**

_____

_____

_____

_____

_____

_____

Special schools are a controversial way of providing education for children with special needs in the UK. Special schools only admit children with special needs and provide adapted facilities and educational provision specifically to meet the needs of children with physical and learning disabilities. Some teachers and families are very positive about special schools and believe that they are the best way of meeting their children's needs. Other parents and teachers are critical of special schools because they believe that these schools disadvantage children by focusing on their special needs rather than on their abilities and educational potential.

9. Describe the advantages or benefits to a child of attending a special school that only admits children with special needs. **(4 marks)**

_____

_____

_____

_____

_____

_____

_____

_____

10. Describe two advantages and two disadvantages of mainstream schooling for children with special needs. **(4 marks)**

   a) Advantages: _____
   _____
   _____
   _____
   _____
   _____

   b) Disadvantages: _____
   _____
   _____
   _____
   _____
   _____
   _____

Glossary

Adoption: the legal process of placing a child with a non-birth parent or parents

Alpha-fetoprotein (AFP): a specialised blood test in pregnancy that can be used to detect some abnormalities

Amniocentesis: a very specialised test, which involves withdrawing a sample of amniotic fluid from the uterus to check for genetic conditions

Amniotic fluid: the liquid that surrounds the foetus in the amniotic sac

Amniotic sac: the sac in which the foetus develops in the uterus

Antenatal: the period between conception and birth

Antibodies: specialised proteins created by the body's immune system to fight off infection

Apgar score: a simple way of assessing a baby's health, immediately after birth, by scoring points for heart rate, breathing, skin colour and tone, and the baby's reactions

Asthma: a non-infectious condition that can be triggered by allergic reactions and causes breathing difficulties

Attachment: a close personal relationship between a parent and child; the important emotional relationship between a baby and its adult carers (also called 'bonding')

Attachment relationship: an emotionally close relationship with a parent or carer through which an infant develops and expresses his or her emotions and sense of security

Attention deficit hyperactivity disorder (ADHD): a condition involving problems with concentration and overactive behaviour

Barrier methods: contraceptives that prevent the sperm from reaching the egg and protect against sexually-transmitted infections (STIs)

Bilingual: the ability to speak two languages

Binovular: non-identical twins conceived from two fertilised ova (eggs)

Birthmark: a blemish on the skin that is formed before birth

Birth plan: a written outline that identifies a couple's preferences for the birth of their baby

Bonding: a strong feeling of connection towards another person, for example, between mother and child

Breech: the position of the baby in the uterus lying bottom or feet first (instead of head first)

British Standards Kitemark: the official mark of quality and reliability (in the form of a Kite symbol) of the British Standards Institute

Caesarean section: a surgical procedure that involves cutting open the uterus to deliver the baby

Casein: the main protein in cows' milk

Cerebral palsy: a group of conditions that are not contagious or progressive, caused by brain damage before or during birth, that result in problems with posture, muscle tone and movement

Cervix: the neck of the uterus (womb)

Chicken pox: an infectious disease caused by a virus that produces very itchy spots

Childcare swaps: this happens when parents take turns to look after one another's children on an informal basis

Childminder: a private sector childcare provider who offers day care for a small number of children in the childminder's own home

Chorionic villus sampling (CVS): a specialised test in pregnancy, which involves taking a sample of the placenta and testing it for Down's syndrome

Cognitive: related to thinking skills and mental processes, like remembering and problem-solving; the scientific term for 'the thought process'

Cohabit: live together

Colic: an attack of stomach pain and excessive crying in a new baby

Colostrum: the first milk produced by the mother's breasts after the birth of the baby

Communication skills: language such as talking, listening and also sign language and lip reading

Conception: fertilisation of the female ovum (egg) by the male sperm

Concepts: ideas that form the building blocks of our knowledge and understanding

Congenital: a condition that is present at birth but isn't necessarily hereditary

Contraception: the use of birth control methods to prevent pregnancy

Contractions: tightening of the muscles of the uterus during labour

Convulsion: uncontrollable contraction of muscles in the body causing jerking movements

Cot death: the sudden and unexplained death of a baby, usually while sleeping

Crèche: a day nursery for pre-school age children and infants, often located in a workplace or shopping centre

Cross-infection: becoming infected with something that originates from a source other than the person themselves

Crowning: the appearance of the baby's head towards the end of labour

Developmental milestones: norms used for monitoring a child's development

Developmental screening tests: regular check-ups to monitor a child's development

Diabetes: a disease that results in high levels of sugar in the blood

Disability: a physical or mental impairment that limits one or more major life activities

Discipline: a system of rules that affect an individual's behaviour and self-control

Down's syndrome: a genetic abnormality that can result in the child having learning difficulties

Early Learning Goals: the targets set for children's learning and development at the end of the Early Years Foundation Stage (at the age of 5)

E-coli: bacteria that can cause food poisoning

Ectopic pregnancy: an embryo developing outside of the uterus

Egocentric: a self-centred person who doesn't take others into account

Embryo: a fertilised ovum from conception to the eighth week of pregnancy

Entonox: a pain-relieving gas that can be breathed in by the woman during labour

Epidural anaesthetic: a pain-relieving injection given into the lower back during labour to numb sensation

Episiotomy: a small cut made to widen the opening of the vagina to ease the delivery of the baby

Exploratory: based on discovering or investigating

Express: to squeeze milk from the breasts, by hand or using a special pump

Extended family: a family that includes parents, children and other relatives (for example, grandparents, uncles, aunts)

EYFS: an acronym for Early Years Foundation Stage

EYFS Profile: a system used to assess the progress of children's learning and development within the EYFS

Family support worker: provides help and guidance with parenting skills and advice about other support services for families

Febrile convulsion: a convulsion caused by high body temperature (above 39 °C)

Fine motor skills: the use of hand and finger movements

Foetal alcohol syndrome: an abnormality that can affect the developing baby if the mother drinks alcohol during pregnancy

Foetus: the developing baby from the eighth week of pregnancy until birth

Folic acid: also known as folate and vitamin B9, this is a B vitamin that is essential for cell growth and reproduction

Fontanelle: the soft spot on top of a baby's head

Food intolerance: a reaction to a food or ingredients in a food product

Food refusal: refusing to eat food offered at mealtimes

Food Standards Agency: a government department responsible for protecting public health in relation to food

Formula milk: milk specially modified for babies

Fostering: the provision of temporary care for a child who is unable to live with his or her own parent(s)

Gastroenteritis: a stomach infection caused by bacteria, with symptoms of extreme vomiting and diarrhoea

Genes: the basic biological unit of inherited ability

Genetic counselling: information and support provided by a specialist counsellor to people who are concerned about the possibility of transmitting birth abnormalities or genetic conditions to their offspring

German measles: a contagious viral disease that can damage foetal development during the first trimester, also known as rubella

Gluten: a type of protein found in wheat, and a common cause of food intolerance in young children

Gonorrhoea: a sexually-transmitted infection

Grammar: the rules used to form words and make sentences

Gross motor skills: the use of large body movements, for example, walking, running, lifting an object or kicking a ball

Guided daily amounts: the amount of calories, sugar, salt and fats that should be eaten daily for a healthy diet

Haemophilia: a group of hereditary genetic disorders that impair the body's ability to control blood clotting (and therefore bleeding)

Hand–eye coordination: the ability to make the hands work together with what the eyes can see

Hand-held notes: detailed notes that record and give the woman access to all the information about the pregnancy

Hazard: a source of danger

Hazardous: something that presents a risk or danger

Head lice: parasites that can live on the human scalp

Health visitor: a qualified health professional who provides help and support to families with young children

Hearing impairment: full or partial loss of hearing, which may be temporary or permanent

HIV: human immunodeficiency virus, which can cause acquired immune deficiency syndrome (AIDS)

Hormones: chemical substances created by glands in the body

Hypothermia: a dangerous condition that occurs when the body temperature falls below 35.5 °C

Immune system: the body's defence system against infection

Immunisation: boosting the immune system by injection with vaccines

Impairment: the loss, lack or absence of some kind of ability

Implantation: the embedding of the fertilised ovum into the wall of the uterus (womb)

Incubation period: the time taken for symptoms to appear after becoming infected with a disease

Incubator: a specialised piece of equipment used to support premature or low birth weight babies

Independent sector: this term is sometimes used to refer to the private and voluntary sectors that are independent of government

Induce: to start labour artificially

Infertility: the inability to conceive a child

Institutionalising: placing a person in an institution

Intellectual: involving the use of the mind

In vitro fertilisation (IVF): an artificial method of conception where fertilisation takes place in a laboratory

Jaundice: a yellowness of the skin and eyes due to the immaturity of a newborn baby's liver

Key person: a childcare provider with special responsibilities for the individual care of specific children within an early years setting

Kindergarten: a pre-school service for children aged 4 to 6 years, usually to prepare them for starting school

Labour: the three stages of giving birth, beginning with the first contractions of the uterus and ending with the delivery of the baby and the placenta

Lactation: the production of breast milk for breastfeeding

Layette: a complete set of clothing for a new baby

Life events: major events in a person's life that affect his or her development and wellbeing

Local authorities: government organisations responsible for the local provision of early years, social care and education services; councils

Local authority: a council

Manipulative task: precise, detailed task that requires the use of small hand and finger movements

Meningitis: a serious infectious disease affecting the meninges around the brain and spinal cord

Menopause: the time in a woman's life when menstrual periods permanently stop

Midwife: a qualified health professional who provides help and support during pregnancy, and during and after birth

Mimicking: copying or imitating another person

Miscarriage: the spontaneous end of a pregnancy and loss of the foetus

Multi-agency working: this involves a team of health, early years and social care workers who are employed by different agencies (care organisations), which work together as part of the same team to provide care for a particular individual or group of people

Muscular dystrophy: a group of hereditary, genetic diseases that weaken the muscles and cause problems with movement

Nappy rash: skin rashes in the areas covered by a baby's nappy

Nature: biologically-based factors or influences

Neonate: the name given to a baby in the first 4 weeks of life

NHS: an acronym for the National Health Service

Non-flammable: not able to burn easily

Nuclear family: two adult parents and their children

Nurture: factors or influences, based on a person's external environment; to take care of

Nurturing: raising a child in a warm, caring manner

Nutrients: substances contained in food that provide nourishment for growth

Obesity: the condition of being extremely overweight; more than 20% above the ideal body weight

Object permanence: understanding that objects still exist, even though they cannot be seen

Obstetrician: a doctor who specialises in the medical care of women during pregnancy and birth

Oestrogen: a female hormone produced by the ovaries

OFSTED: an acronym for the Office for Standards in Education

One-parent family: a family consisting of a single parent and at least one dependent child

Organic: foodstuff which is grown or produced naturally, without any artificial fertilisers, pesticides or hormones

Ovulation: the release of an ovum from the ovary

Paediatrician: a doctor who specialises in the medical care of children

Palmar grasp: using the whole hand to pick up and hold objects

Parasites: living creatures that feed on the human body

Partnership working: typically this involves different organisations working together (as partners) to provide a service

Pethidine: a pain-relieving injection given during labour

Phonic knowledge: learning that involves associating letters with their sounds

Pincer grasp: using the thumb and index finger to pick up and hold small objects

Placenta: part of the uterus that provides blood and nutrients for and transfers waste from the developing foetus; the organ that nourishes the foetus in the uterus

Postnatal depression: a serious form of depression that can affect some women after the birth of the baby

Postnatal period: the first 6 weeks after the birth of the baby

Pre-conceptual: before conception

Pre-eclampsia: a condition in pregnancy that causes high blood pressure, which can be dangerous to the developing foetus

Premature: born before 37 weeks of pregnancy

Premature labour: labour that begins spontaneously before the 37th week of pregnancy

Private sector: this consists of organisations and self-employed care practitioners who charge a fee for their services

Problem-solving skills: the skills children need to figure out how things work, what things do, where things go and why things happen

Progesterone: a female hormone produced in the ovaries

Progestogen: a form of the female hormone progesterone used in contraceptive pills

Prone position: lying on the stomach

Punishment: some form of penalty imposed for unacceptable behaviour

Reconstituted family: a form of step-family in which one or both partners have children from previous relationships

Recuperation: recovery

Regression: going back to an earlier stage of development or behaviour; returning to a former emotional state

Regulate: control or influence

Regulated: governed or controlled

Respite care: care that provides short-term, temporary relief to those caring for children or other relatives

Risk: the chance of loss, damage or injury occurring

Risk assessment: the process of examining whether a toy or other object may injure or harm a child

Rubella: a contagious virus also known as 'German measles' that can cause a miscarriage or serious birth defects if contracted during pregnancy

Safeguarding: protection

Saturated fat: the type of fat found mostly in animal products like butter, linked to an increased risk of heart disease

Separation anxiety: a feeling of strong anxiety and abandonment

Socialisation: the process of teaching (and learning) the attitudes, values and expectations of society

Solitary: doing something alone

Special needs: the additional needs for help and support that a child may have because of health, learning or developmental problems; the additional or further needs for assistance people have because of an illness or disability

Spina bifida: a condition in which the spine of the foetus does not form properly, resulting in loss of sensation and severe muscle weakness in the lower parts of the body

Statutory: relating to the law (statute)

Stigma: a characteristic, behaviour or label that discredits or damages the reputation of a person

Subsidise: to pay part of the cost

Symptoms: changes in the body caused by an illness

Testosterone: the male sex hormone

'Topping and tailing': washing a baby's face, hands, bottom and genital areas

Toxoplasmosis: a disease passed on from contact with cat faeces, which can cause damage to the developing foetus

Transcutaneous electrical nerve stimulation (TENS): a device that blocks pain signals during labour

Trimester: a period in pregnancy, roughly equivalent to 12 weeks

Tripod grasp: using the thumb and first two fingers to hold objects

Ultrasound scan: a test that uses sound waves to create an image of the foetus in the uterus

Umbilical cord: connects the foetus to the placenta

Umbilicus: the navel, where the umbilical cord is attached

Uniovular: identical twins conceived from one fertilised ovum

Ventouse extraction: a procedure that uses a vacuum device to assist the delivery of the baby

Vernix: a white greasy substance that protects the baby's skin in the uterus

Viable: the stage when the foetus is capable of surviving outside of the uterus

Voluntary sector: this consists of large and small organisations that are independent of government and provide services on a not-for-profit basis

Weaning: the process of introducing solid food to a baby's diet

Notes

www.ingramcontent.com/pod-product-compliance
Ingram Content Group UK Ltd.
Pitfield, Milton Keynes, MK11 3LW, UK
UKHW051948180325
456415UK00012B/146